NOT YET CHRISTMAS

IT'S TIME FOR **ADVENT**

A DAILY READER

J. D. Walt

Dave Harrity
Poetry Editor

Scripture quotations are taken from NRSV the Holy Bible: New Revised Standard Version/Division of Christian Education of the National Council of Churches of Christ in the United States of America.—Nashville: Thomas Nelson Publishers, c 1989. Used by permission. All rights reserved.

Scripture quotations marked NIV are taken from THE HOLY BIBLE, NEW INTERNATIONAL VERSION®, NIV® Copyright © 1973, 1978, 1984, 2011 by Biblica, Inc.™ Used by permission. All rights reserved worldwide.

Printed in the United States of America

Hardcover ISBN: 978-1-62824-158-7
Mobi ISBN: 978-1-62824-159-4
ePub ISBN: 978-1-62824-160-0
uPDF ISBN: 978-1-62824-161-7

Library of Congress Control Number: 2014948598

Cover and page design by Brushfire Design Studio

SEEDBED PUBLISHING
Franklin, Tennessee
Seedbed.com
SOWING FOR A GREAT AWAKENING

CONTENTS

PREFACE

A Word to Christian Communities and Those Who Lead Them

It's time . . .

It's time to stop crying in our soup about the consumeristic commercialization of Christmas. Instead of bashing the culture for making Black Friday bigger than Thanksgiving, let's do something different this year. Let's do Advent. Instead of shaming each other for giving more to our children instead of digging wells in Africa, let's give the Holy Spirit room to narrate us into a bigger story, one that might send our hearts to Africa and not just our money. Shame might increase the amount of change we put into the kettles outside the mall this year, but it will not make us the people and communities God intends us to become.

Instead of quibbling over saying "Happy Holidays" instead of "Merry Christmas," let's recover what it means to celebrate Holy Days. Instead of our cheesy slogans about the "Reason for the Season," let's just do the season. Let's joyfully embrace the fact that we will do Advent in the midst of a culture that loves Christmas but doesn't really understand it. But let's not be mad about it. We do not live in a Christian culture. We live in an American culture. Our privileged responsibility is to be real Christians in this particular culture. We need not be against this culture anymore than we need to baptize it. Jesus is not competing with Santa. Let's embrace it by singing along with "Here Comes Santa Claus" and "Jingle Bells." Let's roast chestnuts over an open fire. Let's learn to be a hospitable guest in what can be a hostile culture.

What this culture most needs from the church is real Christians. That's what Advent is designed to do. Advent lifts our hearts to a future of unparalleled possibility and beckons us to awaken from the predictable certainty that our lives have become. Advent rings in a new year, offering Christians once more the chance to begin again. Let us together set our feet on the path of pilgrimage, the way of purposeful wandering.

Advent reverses the tired cliché of Christmas, "The Reason for the Season," by offering us a "Season for the Reason." When the church reclaims Advent, the culture will behold Christmas.

INTRODUCTION

Welcome to Advent

*I don't deny that there should be priests to remind men that they
will one day die. I only say ... it is necessary to have another kind
of priests, called poets, actually to remind men that they are not
dead yet.*

—*G. K. Chesterton*

It's time to return to Advent.

It's time to give prophets a hearing again, listening with the playful
intensity of a child hearing a story for the first time.

It's time to slow down long enough to amble through the intolerable
ambiguity of poems, submitting to a meaning we cannot comprehend
until we surrender our need to control it.

It's time to begin again, only this time with the end in sight, to lift
our eyes first to the clouds on which he will come, before we fix them
on the star of his first arrival.

It's time to teach our children that the grass will wither and the
flower will fade but the Word of the Lord will endure forever.

Advent reminds us of a certain event, a day on the horizon of the
future which will reorder every last molecule of the universe. This
event is the second coming of Jesus Christ. Despite all the uncertain-
ties of timing, this event is a fixed certainty. The message of the gospel:
Do not be afraid. Be prepared.

How This Reader Works

Each of the twenty-five days offers a carefully chosen text from the Bible, each of which the church has read for many centuries during the season of Advent. Following the text, there is a short bit of narration designed to steadily guide the reader along the path of pilgrimage, day by day. Finally, each day closes with a prayer in the form of a poem. J. D. Walt serves as the narrator. Dave Harrity has carefully curated a host of award-winning poets to provide our prayers. The arrangement aims to slow us down, to break pace with the normal routine. We are creating space to behold, to hear a fresh word from the Holy Spirit, to catch a glimpse of a new horizon, to sing the song of the future.

ANTHEM OF ADVENT

It's ironic. The song the church tends to save until Christmas Eve, "Joy to the World," is actually not a Christmas carol. It's an Advent anthem. It's a song about the second coming of Jesus. It's a sign that we've so Christmas-ized Advent that we turn one of the few and precious songs about the Second Advent into a carol for the first Christmas. Take a look:

Joy to the World

Joy to the world, the Lord is come!
Let earth receive her King;
Let every heart prepare him room,
And Heaven and nature sing,
And Heaven and nature sing,
And Heaven, and Heaven, and nature sing.

Joy to the world, the Savior reigns!
Let men their songs employ;
While fields and floods, rocks, hills, and plains
Repeat the sounding joy,
Repeat the sounding joy,
Repeat, repeat, the sounding joy.

No more let sins and sorrows grow,
Nor thorns infest the ground;
He comes to make his blessings flow
Far as the curse is found,
Far as the curse is found,
Far as, far as, the curse is found.

He rules the world with truth and grace,
And makes the nations prove
The glories of his righteousness,
And wonders of his love,
And wonders of his love,
And wonders, wonders, of his love.

—*Isaac Watts*

NOT YET CHRISTMAS

A PRAYER FOR THE OPENING OF ADVENT

Give ear, O Shepherd of Israel, you who lead [your people] like a flock! You who are enthroned upon the cherubim, shine forth.

—PSALM 80:1

From ages past no one has heard, no ear has perceived, no eye has seen any God besides you, who works for those who wait for him.

—ISAIAH 64:4

Come, Holy Spirit, and inaugurate Advent in our midst. Come and open up the book of a new year of our Lord. Lift our hearts to long for your coming and deepen our longing to imagine your kingdom.

We confess—Advent, the season of holy anticipation, has become for us a sign of anxiety. Like Martha, we busy ourselves with so many things, preparing for a celebration of our own design. We confess—our attention has become distraction. Our hearts, minds, and souls are divided as we literally surf the channels of our consumeristic culture. "Yet, O LORD, you are our Father; we are the clay, and you are our potter; we are all the work of your hand" (Isa. 64:8). Begin anew this Advent to shape us. Make us like Mary to sit at the feet of our Lord Jesus and discover the only necessary thing: your Presence. Restore us, O God; let your face shine, that we may be saved. Shape these days of Advent into a season of undivided attention, of holy anticipation.

As we sing of peace on Earth and goodwill to all people, open our ears to hear the mournful songs of a war-torn world: the unquenchable cries of ordinary families like our own whose losses are beyond our ability to comprehend. As we prepare to wrap the countless gifts our children will open on Christmas morning, open our hearts to the countless children for whom Christmas morning will be yet another day to survive. Lead us to respond to you in remembering those who will otherwise receive nothing, who are orphaned, whose parents are dead, distant, or imprisoned. Open our eyes to see those neighbors nearest to us who are lonely, afraid, sick, and suffering. We confess— our lifestyles have become enclaves of escape from the pain and suffering that surrounds us. "Yet, O LORD, you are our Father; we are the clay, and you are our potter; we are all the work of your hand" (Isa. 64:8). Let this year be different, Lord. Shape our attention in these days of Advent into a lifestyle of love for neighbor and the needy.

"Give ear, O Shepherd of Israel, you who lead [your people] like a flock! You who are enthroned upon the cherubim, shine forth" (Ps. 80:1). "O that you would tear open the heavens and come down, so that the mountains would quake at your presence" (Isa. 64:1). As we remember and celebrate the birth of the baby in Bethlehem, let us not forget that the King is returning. We confess—we have made ourselves at home in a world that is not our home. We know a time is coming when the sun will be darkened and the moon will not give us light, when the stars will be falling from heaven, and the powers in the heavens will be shaken. We know the Son of Man will come on the clouds with great power and glory and he will send out his angels to gather his elect from the ends of the earth to the ends of heaven (see Mark 13:24–27). Stir in our hearts a holy anticipation for the world to come, and an undying urgency for the world that is passing away. By your Spirit, make us watchful and wakeful. For, "O LORD, you are our Father; we are the clay, and you are our potter; we are all the work of your hand" (Isa. 64:8).

Come, Holy Spirit, and inaugurate Advent in our midst. Come and open up the book of a new year of our Lord. Hear us as we pray:

Our Father in heaven,

hallowed be your name,

your kingdom come,

your will be done,

    on earth as it is in heaven.

Give us today our daily bread.

And forgive us our debts,

    as we also have forgiven our debtors.

And lead us not into temptation,

    but deliver us from the evil one.

—MATTHEW 6:9–13 NIV

1

IT'S TIME TO REMEMBER THE FUTURE

Be patient, then, brothers and sisters, until the Lord's coming. See how the farmer waits for the land to yield its valuable crop, patiently waiting for the autumn and spring rains. You too, be patient and stand firm, because the Lord's coming is near. Don't grumble against one another, brothers and sisters, or you will be judged. The Judge is standing at the door! Brothers and sisters, as an example of patience in the face of suffering, take the prophets who spoke in the name of the Lord. As you know, we count as blessed those who have persevered. You have heard of Job's perseverance and have seen what the Lord finally brought about. The Lord is full of compassion and mercy.

—JAMES 5:7-11 NIV

It's time that we come to terms with this fact: the return of the Lord is a good thing. Is it not? But you say, there are so many people I know who are not ready for this—the end of all things broken and the fulfillment of all things made new. And so, the Advent question of questions: What about these people you love? Have you spoken to them concerning the end of all things broken and the fulfillment of all things made new? And how about you? Are you ready? If not, there is only one good reason.

It is because you are not sure the return of the Lord is a good thing.

Think about it. The return of the Lord means: No more child slavery. No more sex trade. No more cancer. No more drug addiction. No more tears. No more terrorism. No more war. No more starvation. No more wheelchairs. The sheen of newness everywhere. The contagion of gladness spreading like wildfire.

All of this and more only begins to describe the extremity of the will of God, which is the totality of his love.

Waiting

I will watch and listen;
I will work and pray.
The extremity of Your will
is the totality of Love.

From my winter window,
I look to the yard
covered in fresh snow.

I recall two goldfinches
playing tag on the sunflowers
as I planted
those seedling redbuds
at the edge of our yard
last summer.
Worry eased from my mind
with each small, careful
shovelful of earth.

The totality of Your will
is the extremity of Love.
I will watch and work;
I will pray and listen.

Now the cold has set in
and the sunflowers are gone
and I say to the Lord only this:
there is so much I can't do
and some that I can.
Help me do and help me wait.

Lord who is near
and full of mercy,
if patience is presence,
make me present to now,
to this bleak sky.
Give me the patience
of the goldfinch,
of the child who delights
in plain blades of grass,
in the simple witness of snow.

—*Daniel Bowman Jr.*

2

IT'S TIME TO LEARN TO STAND ON A WORD

"There will be signs in the sun, the moon, and the stars, and on the earth distress among nations confused by the roaring of the sea and the waves. People will faint from fear and foreboding of what is coming upon the world, for the powers of the heavens will be shaken. Then they will see 'the Son of Man coming in a cloud' with power and great glory. Now when these things begin to take place, stand up and raise your heads, because your redemption is drawing near." Then he told them a parable: "Look at the fig tree and all the trees; as soon as they sprout leaves you can see for yourselves and know that summer is already near. So also, when you see these things taking place, you know that the kingdom of God is near. Truly I tell you, this generation will not pass away until all things have taken place. Heaven and earth will pass away, but my words will not pass away. Be on guard so that your hearts are not weighed down with dissipation and drunkenness and the worries of this life, and that day catch you un-expectedly, like a trap. For it will come upon all who live on the face of the whole earth. Be alert at all times, praying that you may have the strength to escape all these things that will take place, and to stand before the Son of Man."

—LUKE 21:25–36

It never failed. Every time I visited the small main street furniture store, the aging widow, the woman of God, asked me the question, "John David, what Word are you standing on today?" She always knew the Word on which she stood. Me? I'm still learning. For on that day when he comes, the Word will be the only place left to stand. And what a spacious, beautiful place it will be.

Now Is the Time to Stand Up

When my heart is heavy,
When my heart is convinced
And my eyes see the signs
That everything is meaningless—
That everything is lost,
I turn to my legs and whisper,
"Now is the time to stand up."

May your words be the earth beneath me.
May your words be a snare
That keep me from the trap
Of believing only what I see,
Of believing the signs
But not the Signifier.

Now is the time to stand up.

—Drew Causey

3
IT'S TIME TO ASK THE DEEPER QUESTIONS

The word that Isaiah son of Amoz saw concerning Judah and Jerusalem. In days to come the mountain of the Lord's house shall be established as the highest of the mountains, and shall be raised above the hills; all the nations shall stream to it. Many peoples shall come and say, "Come, let us go up to the mountain of the Lord, to the house of the God of Jacob; that he may teach us his ways and that we may walk in his paths." For out of Zion shall go forth instruction, and the word of the Lord from Jerusalem. He shall judge between the nations, and shall arbitrate for many peoples; they shall beat their swords into plowshares, and their spears into pruning hooks; nation shall not lift up sword against nation, neither shall they learn war any more. O house of Jacob, come, let us walk in the light of the Lord!

—ISAIAH 2:1–5

It's time to ask the questions: What of my life? Am I fashioning myself as a sword or being fashioned into a plow? I want to be sharpened for the glory of God. I must be bent instead for the glory of the ground. I want to climb the mountain, take the hill, ascend to greatness. I must learn to churn the soil so my children might come after me sowing seeds of Light. What will be my legacy? What do I leave in my wake—a fertile furrow or a monument to myself?

These words are not practical, you say. And you are correct. These words purpose to unshackle us from the false security of a safe existence. You were made for more. You were crafted to express the impractical extravagance of Holy Love.

The Mountain of You

How can I climb the mountain of you Lord?
Where are the dusty cuts carved out?

I've spent most of this life wandering—
sometimes toward, sometimes away—

but always dazed and unsure whether
it's ascent or descent, rise or fall.

Whether rolling in a stream
or falling from a summit,

a stone is a stone is a stone
and I've seen these forms before.

My God, my God—
how will I get to you?

Is it a mountain
and my legs are broken?

Is it a boulder
too heavy for my arms?

Either way, it will not be moved.
This stone feels familiar.

Give me life and roll it quietly away.

—*Dave Harrity*

4

IT'S TIME TO SHED OUR CYNICISM

A shoot will come up from the stump of Jesse; from his roots a Branch will bear fruit. The Spirit of the Lord will rest on him—the Spirit of wisdom and of understanding, the Spirit of counsel and of might, the Spirit of the knowledge and fear of the Lord—and he will delight in the fear of the Lord.

He will not judge by what he sees with his eyes, or decide by what he hears with his ears; but with righteousness he will judge the needy, with justice he will give decisions for the poor of the earth. He will strike the earth with the rod of his mouth; with the breath of his lips he will slay the wicked. Righteousness will be his belt and faithfulness the sash around his waist.

The wolf will live with the lamb, the leopard will lie down with the goat, the calf and the lion and the yearling together; and a little child will lead them. The cow will feed with the bear, their young will lie down together, and the lion will eat straw like the ox. The infant will play near the cobra's den, and the young child will put its hand into the viper's nest. They will neither harm nor destroy on all my holy mountain, for the earth will be filled with the knowledge of the Lord as the waters cover the sea.

In that day the Root of Jesse will stand as a banner for the peoples; the nations will rally to him, and his resting place will be glorious.

—ISAIAH 11:1–10 NIV

It's time to train our eyes to see the beatific vision, to hone our sight on the horizon, to learn to behold the *glorious feast of the future*. In order to do this, we must rid ourselves of the soul's cancer, cynicism. The cynic cloaks himself in the wise disguise of a realist. Truth be told, realism is just another name for a defeated idealism. Cynicism is the bitter fruit of a desecrated imagination. Cynicism treats the sickness of our hopelessness with the topical ointment of our thinly veiled anger.

So why do we rush to those angry, armchair dime-store prophets who can only assuage our fears by blaming the Republicans or the Democrats? Advent calls saying, "Listen to these prophets of the arduous possible. Let them encompass your weary imagination. They offer no easy solutions. They impart vision. We perish without it." That's what cynicism is, dead people who still have a pulse. But remember, a pulse means there's still a possibility.

Will Be Glorious

Tiny as a secret, Lord,
dormant as seeds, you wait

the way we wait for you
to remind us what's cut down

may not be lost forever,
but instead, slowly,

in some hidden center,
cultivating new fruit.

Some mornings our hands
feel kind as orchards, clean as

fleece. Others, we're all
claw, yanked toward the scent

of meat. Tarnish of blood. Lord,
we long for you to lamb us

in our wrath, beast us in our apathy.
For you to bloom out, to be again

the branch—the tree itself and not
the body pinned so terribly there.

We wait, Lord, for you to gather us—
goat and leopard, wolf and calf—

in one noisy, lovely flock. For you
to overcome us, as vines consume

and sweeten a hillside. For you
to wave over the world a banner

of water, washing us whiter
than pearls, finally illuminated.

—*Amy McCann*

5

IT'S TIME TO SING THE OLD SONG

Sing aloud, O daughter Zion; shout, O Israel! Rejoice and exult with all your heart, O daughter Jerusalem! The LORD has taken away the judgments against you, he has turned away your enemies. The king of Israel, the LORD, is in your midst; you shall fear disaster no more. On that day it shall be said to Jerusalem: Do not fear, O Zion; do not let your hands grow weak. The LORD, your God, is in your midst, a warrior who gives victory; he will rejoice over you with gladness, he will renew you in his love; he will exult over you with loud singing as on a day of festival. I will remove disaster from you, so that you will not bear reproach for it. I will deal with all your oppressors at that time. And I will save the lame and gather the outcast, and I will change their shame into praise and renown in all the earth. At that time I will bring you home, at the time when I gather you; for I will make you renowned and praised among all the peoples of the earth, when I restore your fortunes before your eyes, says the LORD.

—ZEPHANIAH 3:14-20

> *"Hope is the ability to hear the music of the future. Faith is having the courage to dance to that song today."*
>
> *—Peter Kuzmich*

At the epicenter of all that exists, a song is playing. Can you hear it? We get something of the song in a short scroll at the very heart of Scripture. It has been called the Song of Songs. And at the core of this song of all songs is a simple chorus of five words. It is the glad song of the Beloved. It is the exultant song of the Bridegroom. It is the expectant song of the future. Five primal Hebrew words: My Beloved Mine. I His.

This is the song of the Holy Spirit, the song of the Father to the Son as the whole of creation was breathed into being by the breath of his Word. This is the song of the Son to the Father as his broken body breathed its last breath of love. This is the song of the Bride back to the Bridegroom as the skies rolled back like a scroll. My beloved mine. I his. It is the soundtrack of the future that plays in the present for all with ears to hear.

A Way in the Wilderness

What is it, LORD, to fear you?
I used to know;
I treasured that gift prominently.

In those days the fear of the LORD kept within me a longing,
a looking for your salvation.

But surely I have neglected your gift,
like the one-use-wonders of Christmases past.

The prophet's words strike today with the force of a hammer
and the tone of spring rain.

Is there a way in the wilderness
yet for me?
Might I hear the songs again
that ring out among the angels,
calling your children to the home of your presence?

Forgive me.
Heal me to the root of my forgetting.
Grant my heart the grin of our ten-month-old,
who still depends on her father's delight.

—Ryan Strebeck

6

IT'S TIME TO TEACH PATIENCE A BIGGER PERSPECTIVE

But do not forget this one thing, dear friends: With the Lord a day is like a thousand years, and a thousand years are like a day. The Lord is not slow in keeping his promise, as some understand slowness. Instead he is patient with you, not wanting anyone to perish, but everyone to come to repentance.

But the day of the Lord will come like a thief. The heavens will disappear with a roar; the elements will be destroyed by fire, and the earth and everything done in it will be laid bare.

Since everything will be destroyed in this way, what kind of people ought you to be? You ought to live holy and godly lives as you look forward to the day of God and speed its coming. That day will bring about the destruction of the heavens by fire, and the elements will melt in the heat. But in keeping with his promise we are looking forward to a new heaven and a new earth, where righteousness dwells.

So then, dear friends, since you are looking forward to this, make every effort to be found spotless, blameless and at peace with him. Bear in mind that our Lord's patience means salvation, just as our dear brother Paul also wrote you with the wisdom that God gave him.

—2 PETER 3:8–15 NIV

We read. We believe. We hope. But, it's been more than two thousand years since he came the first time, 730,000 days! Come on, Jesus! We are ready for the new heaven and the new earth. We are ready for no more suffering, the end of injustice, no more children sold into slavery or the sex trade, no more cancer, no more divorce, no more war. We are ready, Jesus. Aren't you looking forward to this? Two thousand years now, the vigil passed from generation to generation. But we will keep perspective in our patience, for according to your calendar it's only been a couple of days.

The Acceptable Year of the Lord

To proclaim the acceptable year of the Lord

These days, I can barely recognise Christmas in the world—
the plastered advertisements, the banners of sales unfurled.
I strain to see beneath the commercials and product
endorsements, deeply sensing this world is no longer my type.

What year is this exactly? It depends on who you ask.
The year of the dog. The age of Aquarius. The year
of still waiting for the Messiah. All I know is I mark
time by God. I follow the Christian calendar because

I believe in commemoration. I believe in Sabbath weekends,
in holy days serving to give my life meaning and order.
All we want in life is consistency, stability. Let the cycle
be infused with the dependability of the seasons.

With Jesus Christ, we understand the past and the future.
We understand our human place. But it's people who forget.
Unmarked time is the great amnesiac, becoming the colour of air,
a glassy blue, vague to see through. Give us a century.

Give enough time. People forget to mark time by endurance.
Give enough time, and everything trivial settles.
Give enough time, and nothing is so important.
Only faith stands up to time. Only faith can even define it.

—*Nicholas Samaras*

7

IT'S TIME TO PUT ON THE ARMOR OF LIGHT

Besides this, you know what time it is, how it is now the moment for you to wake from sleep. For salvation is nearer to us now than when we became believers; the night is far gone, the day is near. Let us then lay aside the works of darkness and put on the armor of light; let us live honorably as in the day, not in reveling and drunkenness, not in debauchery and licentiousness, not in quarreling and jealousy. Instead, put on the Lord Jesus Christ, and make no provision for the flesh, to gratify its desires.

—ROMANS 13:11–14

The seduction of darkness can be almost overwhelming. Every day the world makes more and more provision for the flesh. What if we took a different approach? What might it mean to stop fighting the darkness and instead simply "put on the armor of light"? What would it look like to "put on the Lord Jesus Christ"?

Just as light displaces darkness, so love displaces sin.

In the Summer's Drought, I Wake and Consider Salvation

No alarm, but the gradual
gathering of rain at 2 a.m.
wake me with a word
clear in my brain: salve.
Drop by cleansing drop,
the words become deluge.
I hear this rain-staccato
echo: go. The surprise
of a summons to head out
and into the holy dark.
Drunkenness, old quarrels,
various hungers of the flesh
slough themselves off, left
tangled in my sheets.
No provision for safety,
I stand almost naked
in the driveway where thunder
surrounds me like a hand.
When three bolts open
the sky, I cannot shut
my eye. And again,
a cataract writes the end
of night, of drought.
My once dead eyes
singed open to see
the dark, wide world
made wet, ready again
for the death of night,
come alive to the fierce
and sudden presences
of light, of day.

—*David Wright*

8

IT'S TIME TO PLOW THE FALLOW GROUND

Give ear, O Shepherd of Israel, you who lead Joseph like a flock! You who are enthroned upon the cherubim, shine forth before Ephraim and Benjamin and Manasseh. Stir up your might, and come to save us! Restore us, O God; let your face shine, that we may be saved. O LORD God of hosts, how long will you be angry with your people's prayers? You have fed them with the bread of tears, and given them tears to drink in full measure. You make us the scorn of our neighbors; our enemies laugh among themselves. Restore us, O God of hosts; let your face shine, that we may be saved.

—PSALM 80:1–7

There's a word for soil that will not grow anything. We call it hardpan. Something happens underneath the surface when ground is not worked for a series of growing seasons. Layers of clay calcify into an impervious shield, preventing water from reaching the subsoil and stopping the possibility of any moisture from seeping back up. The result? No more topsoil to grow anything new. What once was fertile loam becomes something akin to impenetrable concrete.

Hardpan. It's an apt description for the condition of people who have lost touch with their inner life. At times this comes from years of consistent neglect. At other times it can be traced to a crushing event or broken relationship somewhere in the past that is still unresolved. Though it's not a foolproof test and by no means scientific, here's a telling question: When was the last time you cried? It may be time for some subsoiling.

Desert Lament

How will I weep without tears?—
my desert skin, my stone eyes.

I have been drinking salt water so long
my body cracks, hands sting.

The sun has an age, but I will never know it—light always.
What are the ways to melt this metal in myself?

There are songs I used to sing,
but since forgotten all the words.

My God, my God—when will you wake up
and hear the wind scratching from my mouth?

—Dave Harrity

IT'S TIME TO BELIEVE IMPOSSIBLE THINGS

"Blessed be the Lord God of Israel, for he has looked favorably on his people and redeemed them. He has raised up a mighty savior for us in the house of his servant David, as he spoke through the mouth of his holy prophets from of old, that we would be saved from our enemies and from the hand of all who hate us. Thus he has shown the mercy promised to our ancestors, and has remembered his holy covenant, the oath that he swore to our ancestor Abraham, to grant us that we, being rescued from the hands of our enemies, might serve him without fear, in holiness and righteousness before him all our days. And you, child, will be called the prophet of the Most High; for you will go before the Lord to prepare his ways, to give knowledge of salvation to his people by the forgiveness of their sins. By the tender mercy of our God, the dawn from on high will break upon us, to give light to those who sit in darkness and in the shadow of death, to guide our feet into the way of peace."

—LUKE 1:68–79

Just nine months prior, the angelic being named Gabriel, who stands in the presence of God, visited Zechariah in the temple. He brought news that he and his aging wife would bear a child. Zechariah did not believe and he was struck silent by the angel.

Fast forward to the scene of today's text. Can you picture him? There's Zechariah, the man whose tongue the angel silenced. He's holding a sign. It says in big letters, "His name is John." With Zechariah's speech now suddenly restored, the Spirit of God shatters the four hundred years of silence with this prophecy of promise, some of the most cherished words in the history of the world.

The game is back on. The Word of God speaks. These words, they are the fresh indications of his mercy. These words promise the impending movements of his grace.

A Prayer

"This is the living source of all virtuous action: for all
our good acts are acts of consent to the indications
of His mercy and the movements of His grace."
—Thomas Merton, from *No Man Is an Island*

These words, oh Lord; indications:
those things that point out or suggest.

Movements: actions, events. Motions. Rhythms,
even. Yes, we must look back and remember

Your holy covenant as You remembered it.
But how can we serve without fear now?

The indications of Your mercy,
the movements of Your grace.

Guide my senses. Help me notice. Help me see.
What is here? What guides me to peace?

The garret dark against rain clouds.
The train whistle at dusk.

A neighbor rocks on her porch swing;
oxygen enters her lungs from a tank.

The indications of Your mercy,
the movements of Your grace.

A boy with thick glasses rides his red bike
around the block over and over.

A wind rustles the high, thin branches
of the birch. The men at the funeral home

move a casket so matter-of-factly they
nearly bump into the doorframe.

Imagination shapes a poem; fingers record it.

The indications of Your mercy,
the movements of Your grace.

—*Daniel Bowman Jr.*

IT'S TIME TO LISTEN FOR A WORD BEYOND THE VOICES OF OUR TIME

In the fifteenth year of the reign of Emperor Tiberius, when Pontius Pilate was governor of Judea, and Herod was ruler of Galilee, and his brother Philip ruler of the region of Ituraea and Trachonitis, and Lysanias ruler of Abilene, during the high priesthood of Annas and Caiaphas, the word of God came to John son of Zechariah in the wilderness. He went into all the region around the Jordan, proclaiming a baptism of repentance for the forgiveness of sins, as it is written in the book of the words of the prophet Isaiah, "The voice of one crying out in the wilderness: 'Prepare the way of the Lord, make his paths straight. Every valley shall be filled, and every mountain and hill shall be made low, and the crooked shall be made straight, and the rough ways made smooth; and all flesh shall see the salvation of God.'"

—*LUKE 3:1-6*

The emperor of the mighty Roman Empire . . . the governor of the conquered country . . . the rulers of the regions . . . the high priests of Jerusalem . . . John—one of these things is not like the others. But note, the *Word of God* did not come to the powerful elite in their palatial wealth. The *Word of God* came to John, the prophet son of a priest, in the trackless wild.

John the Baptist gets a lot more than honorable mention in the days of Advent. This locust eating, grisly bear of a man does not conjure up images of chestnuts roasting over an open fire. Out of nowhere comes this towering figure who people can only describe by saying words like Elijah and Isaiah.

He is announcing a baptism of repentance. And repentance isn't exactly a word we associate with Christmas, but remember—it's *not Christmas*.

And what, you ask, is a baptism of repentance? Repentance means the realignment of one's life with what matters most. It's a breaking away from and a preparing for. It's the recognition of the mounting holy discontent in the pit of your soul. It's the awakening of anticipation, the storm before the calm.

It's okay to sing the songs of Santa and jingle the bells of the season brewing about us. Nothing could be more important, though, than quietly attending to the repentance called Advent.

Prepare

Soul-breather, Night-breaker, World-making Word
Remake me, now, to see you, O, fearfully!
Foreign and unfamiliar, unsafe. Pour red blood
over the sappiest picture-book portraits my mind can muster.

Self-offerer, Purest Purse-bearer, Re-enslaver
Burn away your blandest face, and shred
the deep banalities of bulletin boards, turn
our heads with your coming, make History.

Right-hand Man of GOD, *Ah! Bright Light-bearer*
Let it be said of us, in the time of this
president, this king, prime minister,
in this time, in time, GOD *came,*

Hill-filler, Mountain-ranger, Mouth of the Rivers
and he sent his man ahead of him (or maybe,
for our confusion, his woman), declaring Jubilee,
oppressors of all kinds cast among the swine,
injustices set right in rather unsurprising ways,
the good stewards rewarded, and the bad theirs,
a kind hand, and with power, will lift the chins
of the down, out, under, without, other, not, and un-,
will pity even us—whose sufferings, let's admit,
are strong but small, like the black ants
that climb our pepper plants, while the hot sun
descends—and bless us!

Spirit-sculptor, Sun-swinger, Dark Matter Master
Reduce us to that waiting, when,
the earth aching, your prophet wades in,
puts hands on shoulder and chest, bids us
hold our breath, before you swallow the world
and remake it as itself, only new.

—Brad Fruhauff

IT'S TIME TO SIFT OUR CLOSETS

John said to the crowds that came out to be baptized by him, "You brood of vipers! Who warned you to flee from the wrath to come? Bear fruits worthy of repentance. Do not begin to say to yourselves, 'We have Abraham as our ancestor'; for I tell you, God is able from these stones to raise up children to Abraham. Even now the ax is lying at the root of the trees; every tree therefore that does not bear good fruit is cut down and thrown into the fire."

And the crowds asked him, "What then should we do?" In reply he said to them, "Whoever has two coats must share with anyone who has none; and whoever has food must do likewise." Even tax collectors came to be baptized, and they asked him, "Teacher, what should we do?" He said to them, "Collect no more than the amount prescribed for you." Soldiers also asked him, "And we, what should we do?" He said to them, "Do not extort money from anyone by threats or false accusation, and be satisfied with your wages."

As the people were filled with expectation, and all were questioning in their hearts concerning John, whether he might be the Messiah, John answered all of them by saying, "I baptize you with water; but one who is more powerful than I is coming; I am not worthy to untie the thong of his sandals. He will baptize you with the Holy Spirit and fire. His winnowing fork is in his hand, to clear his threshing floor and to gather the wheat into his granary; but the chaff he will burn with unquenchable fire."

So, with many other exhortations, he proclaimed the good news to the people.

—LUKE 3:7–18

Two coats. It's quite the call to repentance. I like coats. I must have a dozen coats; one for every possible climate I might face. There's that Banana Republic warm-up coat, and the Barbour all-weather coat, and the Diesel pull-over coat, and the J. Crew Barn coat, and the Mossy Oak camo-hunting coat, and the L. L. Bean denim coat and . . . you get the picture. I like them all so much that when it comes time to give a coat away, I'll go into the way-way-back of the closet and pull out an old one I don't wear anymore.

This year I'm finally going to do it. I'm going to take one of the coats I like, maybe even one of the new ones, and give it away to someone who doesn't have a coat. It's too bad John didn't tell me how many to give away if I had twelve coats.

And you? Have you counted your coats lately? We so often think of repentance as an inner feeling of sorrow over bad behavior and a resolve not to do it again. John says it's a lot bigger than this. When there are people without coats and I have twelve . . . you get the point. Count those coats.

Two Coats

We want to know. We want a set
of step-by-steps directing us,

our future in black-and-white
illustrated instructions finally

composed by someone sympathetic
to our anguish—how desperately we try

to attach the proper knob, make A
meet B, cram the bolt in its narrow,

pre-drilled channel. Is it sin
to own two coats? To gulp

our second, our third serving
of bread? Or, worse, to ask

minor questions of prophets,
who—honed by their intake

of nothing save insects,
Scripture, nectar—can tell us only

how we ought to wait?
What we should do is know

how God can change a stone
into an heir, can prune a vine

to sweeten the eventual swallow,
can sift the heaviest harvest

into what will nourish and what
will burn, while we can do nothing

but salvage a few spare parts, fumble
the assembly, jerry-rig our mismatched,

junk-drawer hearts to love a little
better than we ever thought we could.

—*Amy McCann*

IT'S TIME FOR REPENTANCE TO BE MORE ABOUT ASPIRATIONS THAN FAILURES

I thank my God every time I remember you, constantly praying with joy in every one of my prayers for all of you, because of your sharing in the gospel from the first day until now. I am confident of this, that the one who began a good work among you will bring it to completion by the day of Jesus Christ. It is right for me to think this way about all of you, because you hold me in your heart, for all of you share in God's grace with me, both in my imprisonment and in the defense and confirmation of the gospel. For God is my witness, how I long for all of you with the compassion of Christ Jesus. And this is my prayer, that your love may overflow more and more with knowledge and full insight to help you to determine what is best, so that in the day of Christ you may be pure and blameless, having produced the harvest of righteousness that comes through Jesus Christ for the glory and praise of God.

—PHILIPPIANS 1:3–11

Repentance. How did such a good word get such a bad rap? The word "repent" conjures up decisively negative images of doomsday preachers shouting on street corners. But what if the word is positive? What if repentance is more about turning toward something really good? Repent means reorienting our highest aspirations toward the best thing imaginable. We were created for lives of inestimable goodness. That's why Paul prays that our love may overflow more and more with knowledge and depth of insight so we can determine what is the very best.

Repentance. It's about holy love.

A Lament for What Is Best

How long Lord will You allow us to lower the bar?
How long will You permit us to reduce discipleship
down to this sticky syrup of mere conversion?

Our greedy hands withhold the broken bread and shed blood.
Our mouths are full of barbed wire. Our feet carry us
always to the places of comfort and ease.

All the world enters our eyes upside down. But You
Oh Lord made the brain to turn it, to orient life toward
what is best. Deliver us from arrogant, unthinking certainty.

Save us from ignorant addiction to inalienable
rights and all of our piled up offences and slights.
Make us to walk in the way of our Lord Jesus Christ.

Press our hands into the rich soil of creation and harvest
the Good News of His character grown in us on Earth
as it is in Heaven. May it be so.

—John Ballenger

IT'S TIME TO QUESTION OUR ASSUMPTIONS ABOUT THE WAY GOD WORKS

When John heard in prison what the Messiah was doing, he sent word by his disciples and said to him, "Are you the one who is to come, or are we to wait for another?" Jesus answered them, "Go and tell John what you hear and see: the blind receive their sight, the lame walk, the lepers are cleansed, the deaf hear, the dead are raised, and the poor have good news brought to them. And blessed is anyone who takes no offense at me."

As they went away, Jesus began to speak to the crowds about John: "What did you go out into the wilderness to look at? A reed shaken by the wind? What then did you go out to see? Someone dressed in soft robes? Look, those who wear soft robes are in royal palaces. What then did you go out to see? A prophet? Yes, I tell you, and more than a prophet. This is the one about whom it is written, 'See, I am sending my messenger ahead of you, who will prepare your way before you.' Truly I tell you, among those born of women no one has arisen greater than John the Baptist; yet the least in the kingdom of heaven is greater than he."

—MATTHEW 11:2-11

Our assumptions about how things should turn out can be blinding. Even more dangerously, these assumptions easily solidify into expectations and unmet expectations are the seeds of future bitterness. Divorce, cancer, bankruptcy, death, etc., weren't supposed to happen. We did everything right, followed Jesus, obeyed God's will. How can this be happening?

Isn't this John's quandary? The child of great promise, forerunner of the Messiah, and prophet of greatest renown sits in a prison cell wondering if he wasted his life. Surely there has to be someone else coming.

We want God on our terms, or we don't want him at all. That's why so often it takes one of life's unforeseen train wrecks to open our eyes to the perspective of divine grace. We tend to meet up with God when we find ourselves backed into a corner with nowhere else to turn. These unwanted moments when we cannot change the reality we face offer the most profound possibilities of true life change.

It may be precisely because the situation cannot change that everything else can. Have you ever heard someone say cancer was the best thing that ever happened to them?

Questions

If, Lord, for your sake, I gave away
my thumbs, my eyes, my keys, half my insides;

if, at your word, I wore wool against my skin
and fed on cicadas and wild, poisonous mushrooms;

if, nudged by some flicker some place near my liver
I spoke a faithful, unironic word;

might I, when the nights grew cold, wonder
if you still cared for me like those you keep in houses;

could I, should the judge come after me, accusing,
remember those preserved through fire, blindness, treachery?

Would I dare blame another, in my place, if he sent to one
with more authority, seeking greater certainties?

Or could I, armed with such a truth, bear up in praise
as my Savior turned his back, left me least among the least,

and walked away, while a servant polishes steel and bears
a plate of brass to please spiteful queen?

—*Brad Fruhauff*

14

IT'S TIME TO DE-SENTIMENTALIZE CHRISTMAS

How can we thank God enough for you in return for all the joy that we feel before our God because of you? Night and day we pray most earnestly that we may see you face to face and restore whatever is lacking in your faith. Now may our God and Father himself and our Lord Jesus direct our way to you. And may the Lord make you increase and abound in love for one another and for all, just as we abound in love for you. And may he so strengthen your hearts in holiness that you may be blameless before our God and Father at the coming of our Lord Jesus with all his saints.

—1 THESSALONIANS 3:9–13

Advent is a key strategy to de-sentimentalize Christmas. Why is this needed? Sentimentality steals the holiness of Christmas and counterfeits its love. Christmas threatens the human condition with the antidote of holy love. Love is not sentimental. Love is not nostalgic. Love is not self-serving. Love is not proud. Love is not easily angered. Love is patient. Love is kind. Love always protects, always trusts, always hopes, always perseveres. Love never fails. That's why this prayer from Scripture means so much: "May the Lord make you increase and abound in love for one another and for all. . . . And may he so strengthen your hearts in holiness that you may be blameless before our God and Father at the coming of our Lord Jesus with all his saints."

Abounding in love . . . strong in holiness. Now, how about changing those second-person pronouns to first person (i.e., from "you" to "me" and "my") and make it your mantra today.

For My Brethren

Lord, ignite my joy for my brethren—
not tolerance, but love (abounding at that!)
for the teenager glaring through hot pink bangs,
for the sagging old lady babbling about her cat.
For the man who snores and drools in the pew,
and for the girl who flutters her hands
during worship, making me wish I'd stayed home.

Give me love for the drunk who returns
every week barely clinging to your hem,
for the righteous one with eyebrows frozen in shock.
For your followers on TV picketing the other side,
dripping in diamonds or wound round with hemp.
Hymn-slingers and praise-song teamsters,
priests who genuflect over the sacred host,

and tattooed ushers ripping off hunks of French bread.
For pre-trib, post-trib, and all tribs strange;
young earth, old earth, and those who wish they'd never arrived
but wipe Jesus' feet with their tears just the same.
Lord, let me see them for who they are, face to face,
lovely in limbs, and lovely in eyes not yours,
but You, You, You, abounding.

—*Tania Runyan*

The italicized line is from Gerard Manley Hopkins' poem,
"As Kingfishers Catch Fire."

IT'S TIME TO CONSIDER ULTIMATE THINGS

Comfort, comfort my people, says your God. Speak tenderly to Jerusalem, and proclaim to her that her hard service has been completed, that her sin has been paid for, that she has received from the LORD's hand double for all her sins.

A voice of one calling: "In the wilderness prepare the way for the LORD; make straight in the desert a highway for our God. Every valley shall be raised up, every mountain and hill made low; the rough ground shall become level, the rugged places a plain. And the glory of the LORD will be revealed, and all people will see it together. For the mouth of the LORD has spoken."

A voice says, "Cry out." And I said, "What shall I cry?"

"All people are like grass, and all their faithfulness is like the flowers of the field. The grass withers and the flowers fall, because the breath of the LORD blows on them. Surely the people are grass. The grass withers and the flowers fall, but the word of our God endures forever."

You who bring good news to Zion, go up on a high mountain. You who bring good news to Jerusalem, lift up your voice with a shout, lift it up, do not be afraid; say to the towns of Judah, "Here is your God!" See, the Sovereign LORD comes with power, and he rules with a mighty arm.

See, his reward is with him, and his recompense accompanies him. He tends his flock like a shepherd: He gathers the lambs in his arms and carries them close to his heart; he gently leads those that have young.

—ISAIAH 40:1–11 NIV

Forsake the tiring routines of prosperity. Go to the nearest ATM and withdraw one hundred dollars. With the cash in hand, go into a convenience store, one you rarely or never visit. Walk up to the cash register and hand the money to the attendant behind the counter. Tell them you want them to have this. Leave. Don't go back. And never tell a soul, save the few friends who agree to do it with you. The money was destined to perish this very year. The gift will last forever.

Now, take out a pen and paper, a daily journal, but nothing electronic. Write these words until they fill up a page: "The grass withers and the flowers fall, but the Word of the Lord endures forever. The grass withers and the flowers fall, but the Word of the Lord endures forever. The grass withers and the flowers fall, but the Word of the Lord endures forever. The grass withers and the flowers fall, but the Word of the Lord endures forever. The grass withers and the flowers fall, but the Word of the Lord endures forever. . . .

A Wilderness Voice

Father, Shepherd of Israel,
teach me a wilderness voice, one
whose vocal chords have no music or mind
of their own but call out, "What shall I cry?"

For even my prayers lack power
lest they be inhabited by yours.
Yes, I finally know, my life fades
like the flower of the field.

I am an annual whose only comfort
is the promise of being planted
in the Perennial Life,
the ground of your Word.

—J. D. Walt

16

IT'S TIME FOR A REFRESHER COURSE ON THE MEANING OF HOLINESS

The desert and the parched land will be glad; the wilderness will rejoice and blossom. Like the crocus, it will burst into bloom; it will rejoice greatly and shout for joy. The glory of Lebanon will be given to it, the splendor of Carmel and Sharon; they will see the glory of the LORD, the splendor of our God.

Strengthen the feeble hands, steady the knees that give way; say to those with fearful hearts, "Be strong, do not fear; your God will come, he will come with vengeance; with divine retribution he will come to save you."

Then will the eyes of the blind be opened and the ears of the deaf unstopped. Then will the lame leap like a deer, and the mute tongue shout for joy. Water will gush forth in the wilderness and streams in the desert. The burning sand will become a pool, the thirsty ground bubbling springs. In the haunts where jackals once lay, grass and reeds and papyrus will grow.

And a highway will be there; it will be called the Way of Holiness; it will be for those who walk on that Way. The unclean will not journey on it; wicked fools will not go about on it. No lion will be there, nor any ravenous beast; they will not be found there.

But only the redeemed will walk there, and those the LORD has rescued will return.

They will enter Zion with singing; everlasting joy will crown their heads. Gladness and joy will overtake them, and sorrow and sighing will flee away.

—ISAIAH 35:1–10 NIV

What if holiness is not what we thought? What if holiness means blind eyes open, deaf ears hearing, lame people leaping, and mute tongues singing? What if holiness means water springing up in the desert, pools of refreshment in the place of arid sand? If so, this means holiness is actually relief; a reversal of broken conditions and situations. This means holiness is love. This means the Way of Holiness looks like a viral movement of concentrated love.

Prayer of the Woman at the Well

If only the bones of my hands
could perceive the dignity extended and restored
to me in this exchange.
Water for living water.

The shame of what I have done in the world,
the bitterness for what it has done to me,
pulled up from this ancient well,
laid bare and washed clean.

You have come Lord and restored me.
You will come Lord, I groan with hope.
You come Lord into the desert
and my soul has burst into bloom!

—John Ballenger

17

IT'S TIME TO RECALIBRATE OUR PACE

To you, O Lord, I lift up my soul. O my God, in you I trust; do not let me be put to shame; do not let my enemies exult over me. Do not let those who wait for you be put to shame; let them be ashamed who are wantonly treacherous. Make me to know your ways, O Lord; teach me your paths. Lead me in your truth, and teach me, for you are the God of my salvation; for you I wait all day long. Be mindful of your mercy, O Lord, and of your steadfast love, for they have been from of old. Do not remember the sins of my youth or my transgressions; according to your steadfast love remember me, for your goodness' sake, O Lord! Good and upright is the Lord; therefore he instructs sinners in the way. He leads the humble in what is right, and teaches the humble his way. All the paths of the Lord are steadfast love and faithfulness, for those who keep his covenant and his decrees.

—PSALM 25:1–10

Have you ever waited for that call from the doctor's office with results of the tests? Have you ever waited for hours in miles of stalled traffic on the interstate? Then there are the checkout lines at the retail outlets within a week of Christmas. How about a traffic light? Have you ever waited for three entire minutes for a light to turn? Then there's the Internet. Have you ever waited for more than thirty seconds for a website to load?

Why do we hate to wait? Is it that we are too busy or too important? Waiting takes us out of control of the situation. Waiting reminds us that someone else is in control. Waiting humbles us. What if the "paths of the Lord" are more about pace than destination? What if our days became exercises in waiting on the Lord, as in, "for you I wait all day long." How about we take all those occasions in the coming days where we find ourselves waiting and we consider in the midst of it all that we are waiting on the Lord.

Ode to the Holy Ghost

Holy shadow, blessed garment of salted light,
I cannot delve deep enough into water
or net meaning from studying the width of scars,
those canals where I exist apart from you.

Draw my dust across the spaces where I might
combust into the living Word, might wake
one morning with the resolve I never mistake,
the passion I've learned not to fight,

but roll through the center of its tide. Pardon
what charges haunt me and create in me
a refinery. Wrap me in the Word, its balm
until my enemies quake in what's defined,

my cobbled road repaired brick by brick,
the hands of a vandal aligned by design.

—Jae Newman

18

IT'S TIME TO DEAL WITH OUR ANXIETY

Rejoice in the Lord always; again I will say, Rejoice. Let your gentleness be known to everyone. The Lord is near. Do not worry about anything, but in everything by prayer and supplication with thanksgiving let your requests be made known to God. And the peace of God, which surpasses all understanding, will guard your hearts and your minds in Christ Jesus.

—PHILIPPIANS 4:4–7

On a sheet of paper make two columns. Label the left column, "Things That Are Bringing Me Joy." Label the right column, "Things That Are Causing Me Anxiety." Take a few minutes to reflect and list out everything you can think of in those two columns. You have likely not done this in a while. You may have never done it at all. It is so important to get these things out of the shadows of our lives and into the light. Start with the left column and literally read them aloud.

Now one at a time, say, "Father, I thank you for _____, and I rejoice in you. Again, I take joy in you." Rejoicing in the Lord and in his blessings has a way of magnifying our blessings and joy. Now read the list on the right column aloud one at a time as a prayer to God. "Father, I give you _____, and I ask you to _____."

In the wake of this work, note the gentleness with which the Spirit is calming your being. We are empty of anxiety and full of joy. This is the life God intends for us to live all the time.

Aren't you glad it's not Christmas yet? Advent wills to rob Christmas of all its anxiety and replace it with pure joy.

Confession in the Key of Kenosis

I am the one who has not
rejoiced, always, and again
I will say, is not, rejoicing.

Hardly ever my gentleness
is known, even to me, and not,
certainly, to my children. Strangers
report to have seen it on Tuesday
in the library. I do not confirm
this sighting.

But I have catalogued
my every worry about everything,
my requests made known in the sharp,
carping voice on my blog. By supplication
and prayer I claim to have been
deserted. I say it again, deserted, justly.

And still, the Lord
stays near, alert for the stingiest rejoicing, his key
ready in his unclenched hand. Unlock, Heart-Guard,
my chest's dark vessel. Empty me of my treasured
losses. And again, I say, make it emptier, until,
for rejoicing, a space large enough to echo appears.

—*David Wright*

19

IT'S TIME TO NAME OUR HOLY DISCONTENT

The days are surely coming, says the Lord, when I will fulfill the promise I made to the house of Israel and the house of Judah. In those days and at that time I will cause a righteous Branch to spring up for David; and he shall execute justice and righteousness in the land. In those days Judah will be saved and Jerusalem will live in safety. And this is the name by which it will be called: "The Lord is our righteousness."

—JEREMIAH 33:14–16

Holy discontent. That's when it begins. When we can finally be honest enough with ourselves to say something like, "There must be more to life than this," or "I'm sick and tired of being sick and tired," or "I have everything I ever wanted, but I still haven't found what I'm looking for." Our contentment with that which does not satisfy slowly lulls us into a slumber many never awaken from. Holy discontent may be the best gift prosperity can give us, for it cracks the door to the kind of room we thought was too good to be true.

It's time to name it. Stop denying that gnawing sense of need just beneath the surface. Stop feeding it with more food or drink or entertainment or toys or trips or new companions. This only increases our appetite for the things that can never satisfy. The difference between a crisis and an awakening is the way we deal with our discontent. It can lead us to holy ground or drive us into the pit of hell.

Here's a dare. Take a minute today and complete this sentence in writing: "The thing I am truly longing for in my life is . . ."

Not Forgotten

Lord, we've stooped down and
watched over this patch of dirt,
waiting for a sign of movement,
longer than any of us care to admit.
There's a seed down in there,
so we've been told and
so we believe,
but would it be too much
to ask for *something*?
A fragile sprout;
a single green shoot.
Anything to let us know that,
deep down in that splendid darkness,
promises are moving toward fullness.

That we haven't been forgotten.

—*Rod Dixon*

20

IT'S TIME TO RE-SEE THE SIGNS

*Again the L*ORD *spoke to Ahaz, "Ask the L*ORD *your God for a sign, whether in the deepest depths or in the highest heights."*

*But Ahaz said, "I will not ask; I will not put the L*ORD *to the test. "*

*Then Isaiah said, "Hear now, you house of David! Is it not enough to try the patience of humans? Will you try the patience of my God also? Therefore the Lord himself will give you a sign: [**BEHOLD!**] The virgin will conceive and give birth to a son, and will call him Immanuel. He will be eating curds and honey when he knows enough to reject the wrong and choose the right, for before the boy knows enough to reject the wrong and choose the right, the land of the two kings you dread will be laid waste.*

—ISAIAH 7:10–16 NIV

Over the days leading up to Christmas, a watchword will present itself in clear fashion. The word? *Behold.* The Greek word we translate as "behold" is *idou.* In most instances, the short Greek word *idou* is simply not translated. For some reason, many modern translators of the most popular versions of the Bible have chosen to leave this word out of our English versions. Can you see the irony? The word meant to alert us to pay special attention to what follows is omitted. Might this, in part, explain some of our failure to acknowledge the vast depth of certain occasions? One no longer looks when they think they have seen; hence our need to be reminded over and again to "Behold!" In order for you, the reader, to feel the effect of this curious and critical omission, I have elected to insert the omitted word, as [Behold]. It is intended to have a jarring effect.

Behold is a very important word. It has the effect of a group of children standing in the middle of a busy intersection wildly waving their arms in order to stop traffic and get passersby to pay attention to what is unfolding just off the well-worn path.

This tiny, overlooked Bible word means "to pay attention," bringing every faculty of our perception into submission to the events unfolding in the world-making wonder of the Word of God.

A sign, whether in the deepest depths or the highest heights. Christmas is all at once a sign both in the deepest depths and the highest heights. Advent prepares us for the apparent contradiction.

A virgin with child? For her, that would be the deepest depths. Pregnant with the Son of God by the power of the Holy Spirit? For us, that would be the highest heights.

"Glory to God in the highest," the angels will soon sing, because glory came down to the lowest. Christmas will show us in sketch what the cross will reveal in full technicolor: a sign both in the deepest depths and the highest heights.

Prayer for the Evening Commute

Snow falling on this familiar route after dark,
hymn after hymn remain
bound in blossom.

Let this silence last. Let it open into the first,
perhaps the only moment,
where what I want to say knows better
and remains unsaid. Let shallow bruises,
constellations of my walk with and without You,
rise as Braille buttons, guideposts
to splint in the sign foretold.

Hone my silver promises, the ones
bore of slithered lies and pride,
because You are the Way, the Truth,
the air rising in my side
as a punch sifts my lungs speechless,

Your presence immediate, radiant
breathlessness unfolding as gasps,
doubt singed by the yoke assigned
to disintegrate mile after mile.

—Jae Newman

21

IT'S TIME TO REVISIT FIRST THINGS

In the sixth month the angel Gabriel was sent by God to a town in Galilee called Nazareth, to a virgin engaged to a man whose name was Joseph, of the house of David. The virgin's name was Mary. And he came to her and said, "Greetings, favored one! The Lord is with you." But she was much perplexed by his words and pondered what sort of greeting this might be. The angel said to her, "Do not be afraid, Mary, for you have found favor with God. [Behold!], you will conceive in your womb and bear a son, and you will name him Jesus. He will be great, and will be called the Son of the Most High, and the Lord God will give to him the throne of his ancestor David. He will reign over the house of Jacob forever, and of his kingdom there will be no end." Mary said to the angel, "How can this be, since I am a virgin?" The angel said to her, "The Holy Spirit will come upon you, and the power of the Most High will overshadow you; therefore the child to be born will be holy; he will be called Son of God. [Behold!] your relative Elizabeth in her old age has also conceived a son; and this is the sixth month for her who was said to be barren. For nothing will be impossible with God." Then Mary said, "[Behold!] Here am I, the servant of the Lord; let it be with me according to your word." Then the angel departed from her.

—LUKE 1:26–38

To behold means to perceive something beyond comprehending. It is the convergence of hearing and sight, where eyes and ears work together to receive a vision.

Mary shows us what it looks like. When we behold something of the ways of God the Holy Spirit ushers us into the realm where "Nothing is impossible with God." These gifted moments tend to invite responses like, "May it be to me according to your word."

If we had to boil the nature of faith down to a couple of essentials, I think they would be these two:

1. "Nothing is impossible with God."
2. "May it be to me according to your word."

After the Annunciation

She couldn't sleep.
Lightning flickered in her head.
Her toes curled and uncurled.

Strange how the world
slumps on as usual, she thought.
Same brown mountains outside,
same cattle herd of snores
from her father.

But even she
couldn't think of angels now,
nor bellies nor saviors
nor blood. Just the images
from yesterday, when she walked
through the marketplace
and knew nothing.

The leprous old woman
crouched outside the city gate,
fingertips dissolving
like bread in the rain.

Two skeletal boys
poking through the mud
for shreds of fish.

Bruised and bejeweled
prostitutes hovering
by the leering vegetable vendors.

Everyone who is probably
lying awake like me, she thought.
Feeling too much. Wondering
why they have been chosen.
Waiting for the world
to start over.

—*Tania Runyan*

22

IT'S TIME TO DO HARD THINGS

Now the birth of Jesus the Messiah took place in this way. When his mother Mary had been engaged to Joseph, but before they lived together, she was found to be with child from the Holy Spirit. Her husband Joseph, being a righteous man and unwilling to expose her to public disgrace, planned to dismiss her quietly.

But just when he had resolved to do this, [Behold!] an angel of the Lord appeared to him in a dream and said, "Joseph, son of David, do not be afraid to take Mary as your wife, for the child conceived in her is from the Holy Spirit. She will bear a son, and you are to name him Jesus, for he will save his people from their sins."

All this took place to fulfill what had been spoken by the Lord through the prophet: "[Behold!] the virgin shall conceive and bear a son, and they shall name him Emmanuel," which means, "God is with us."

When Joseph awoke from sleep, he did as the angel of the Lord commanded him; he took her as his wife, but had no marital relations with her until she had borne a son; and he named him Jesus.

—MATTHEW 1:18–25

The story of Christmas has absolutely zero in common with our snow globe nativity set. Consider Joseph. Here was an ordinary guy, excited about marrying the girl of his dreams. And in an afternoon everything imploded. In his mind, it was over. The dignified exit strategy was all but done. Then there was the dream.

Joseph did the hard thing. Life would not get easier. His hope for a normal life was over. Later would come yet another dream warning him to take his family and leave the country to avoid genocide. This son who was not his son would cost him everything. Joseph died to his dreams for the sake of the greater dream. Joseph, without doubt, is the most underrated and under-celebrated member of the cast of the story of Jesus. He did the hard thing.

Were he among us, he would likely offer us this advice: "Do hard things. It's worth it. And remember, sometimes what seems to be righteous may not always be right."

To the One I Almost Left

To the one I almost left
To save my own skin:
What seems to be righteous
May not always be right.
I had a dream about you.
We took turns teaching
One another a song;
I knew the tune
But only you could carry it.
When I woke up,
The melody was loud—
Louder in my waking
Than in my sleeping.
Your song woke me up
And now keeps me awake.

I will sing this song
Until I see you
Face to face
And you take the song
Back for all of us.

—*Drew Causey*

23
IT'S TIME TO BEHOLD THE MIRACLE

In those days Mary set out and went with haste to a Judean town in the hill country, where she entered the house of Zechariah and greeted Elizabeth. When Elizabeth heard Mary's greeting, the child leaped in her womb. And Elizabeth was filled with the Holy Spirit and exclaimed with a loud cry, "Blessed are you among women, and blessed is the fruit of your womb. And why has this happened to me, that the mother of my Lord comes to me? For [Behold!] as soon as I heard the sound of your greeting, the child in my womb leaped for joy. And blessed is she who believed that there would be a fulfillment of what was spoken to her by the Lord." And Mary said, "My soul magnifies the Lord, and my spirit rejoices in God my Savior, for he has looked with favor on the lowliness of his servant. [Behold!] Surely, from now on all generations will call me blessed; for the Mighty One has done great things for me, and holy is his name. His mercy is for those who fear him from generation to generation. He has shown strength with his arm; he has scattered the proud in the thoughts of their hearts. He has brought down the powerful from their thrones, and lifted up the lowly; he has filled the hungry with good things, and sent the rich away empty. He has helped his servant Israel, in remembrance of his mercy, according to the promise he made to our ancestors, to Abraham and to his descendants forever."

—LUKE 1:39–55

God crafted the human soul for the purpose of beholding. To behold something means to see it and magnify it with your soul. Your soul is a magnifying glass. The question: What is your soul magnifying?

Hear Mary, "My soul magnifies the Lord." We magnify what we see. Your spirit is an amplifier. The question: What is your spirit amplifying? Hear Mary, "And my spirit rejoices in God my Savior." We amplify what we hear. Seeing with the soul. Hearing with the spirit. Eyes to see? Ears to hear? When the Holy Spirit captures the totality of our attention, unifying our hearing and seeing, where magnification meets amplification.

We Behold

Father,
Last summer I saw a sight
forever now with me.

My daughter, Lily, magnifying glass
in hand, focused the warm beam
of the radiant star onto her exploring hat,
burning, smoldering a tiny hole.

As the invisible blaze burned clean through,
the children jumped for joy in the driveway.

Then she burned another hole and another,
each in succession, connected to the last.

Wow! I thought, *she's ruined a perfectly good hat.*
Until I looked closer and saw the pattern in the still smoking holes
spelling "Lily," the letters of her name.

Today in the chill of the solstice of winter,
as the Sun stands still on the southern horizon
the skies seem to shout at me, "Behold!"

And those seeds of summer sprout in the garden
of my mind and I see meaning in each one.

And so I ask you to let it be with me,
according to your Word,
that I would walk in the blessedness of belief.

—*J. D. Walt*

24

IT'S TIME TO GO TO BETHLEHEM

In those days Caesar Augustus issued a decree that a census should be taken of the entire Roman world. (This was the first census that took place while Quirinius was governor of Syria.) And everyone went to their own town to register.

So Joseph also went up from the town of Nazareth in Galilee to Judea, to Bethlehem the town of David, because he belonged to the house and line of David. He went there to register with Mary, who was pledged to be married to him and was expecting a child. While they were there, the time came for the baby to be born, and she gave birth to her firstborn, a son. She wrapped him in cloths and placed him in a manger, because there was no guest room available for them.

And there were shepherds living out in the fields nearby, keeping watch over their flocks at night. An angel of the Lord appeared to them, and the glory of the Lord shone around them, and they were terrified. But the angel said to them, "Do not be afraid. [Behold!] I bring you good news that will cause great joy for all the people. Today in the town of David a Savior has been born to you; he is the Messiah, the Lord. This will be a sign to you: You will find a baby wrapped in cloths and lying in a manger."

Suddenly a great company of the heavenly host appeared with the angel, praising God and saying,

"Glory to God in the highest heaven, and on earth peace to those on whom his favor rests."

When the angels had left them and gone into heaven, the shepherds said to one another, "Let's go to Bethlehem and see this thing that has happened, which the Lord has told us about."

So they hurried off and found Mary and Joseph, and the baby, who was lying in the manger. When they had seen him, they spread the word concerning what had been told them about this child, and all who heard it were amazed at what the shepherds said to them. But Mary treasured up all these things and pondered them in her heart. The shepherds returned, glorifying and praising God for all the things they had heard and seen, which were just as they had been told.

—*LUKE 2:1–20 NIV*

The time has come. The kingdom of God is at hand. Advent has prepared us well. We are ready. "Let's go to Bethlehem and see this thing that has happened." It's Christmas!

Among Us

Jesus, Eternal Creator,
I celebrate You as the Living Word,
the Fire that came to illuminate
the shadowy places of our fallen world.

I rejoice that You came to dwell
among us and show Yourself to us,
that You do not leave us to ourselves
to wander in the darkness.

As John was sent to speak of Your nature,
and testify of Who You are,
I ask that you send me.
I will carry Your light to the dark places,

that eyes blinded as mine once were will be opened.
I will bear Your heart to abandoned corners
and neglected alleyways and share the joy
of being Your child.

Use my humble steps to reflect Your grace,
my willing lips to let loose Your glory,
In Your name, I pray. Amen.

—Amy L. George

25

IT'S TIME FOR CHRISTMAS

In the beginning was the Word, and the Word was with God, and the Word was God. He was with God in the beginning. Through him all things were made; without him nothing was made that has been made. In him was life, and that life was the light of all mankind. The light shines in the darkness, and the darkness has not overcome it.

There was a man sent from God whose name was John. He came as a witness to testify concerning that light, so that through him all might believe. He himself was not the light; he came only as a witness to the light.

The true light that gives light to everyone was coming into the world. He was in the world, and though the world was made through him, the world did not recognize him. He came to that which was his own, but his own did not receive him. Yet to all who did receive him, to those who believed in his name, he gave the right to become children of God—children born not of natural descent, nor of human decision or a husband's will, but born of God.

The Word became flesh and made his dwelling among us. We have seen his glory, the glory of the one and only Son, who came from the Father, full of grace and truth.

—JOHN 1:1–14 NIV

MERRY CHRISTMAS!

"Hark! The Herald Angels Sing"

Hark! The herald angels sing,
"Glory to the newborn King;
Peace on earth, and mercy mild,
God and sinners reconciled!"
Joyful, all ye nations rise,
Join the triumph of the skies;
With th'angelic host proclaim,
"Christ is born in Bethlehem!"

Refrain:
Hark! the herald angels sing,
"Glory to the newborn King!"

Christ, by highest Heav'n adored;
Christ the everlasting Lord;
Late in time, behold Him come,
Offspring of a virgin's womb.
Veiled in flesh the Godhead see;
Hail th'incarnate Deity,
Pleased with us in flesh to dwell,
Jesus our Emmanuel.

Hail the heav'nly Prince of Peace!
Hail the Sun of Righteousness!
Light and life to all He brings,
Ris'n with healing in His wings.
Mild He lays His glory by,
Born that man no more may die.
Born to raise the sons of earth,
Born to give them second birth.

Come, Desire of nations, come,
Fix in us Thy humble home;
Rise, the woman's conqu'ring Seed,
Bruise in us the serpent's head.
Now display Thy saving power,
Ruined nature now restore;
Now in mystic union join
Thine to ours, and ours to Thine.

Adam's likeness, Lord, efface,
Stamp Thine image in its place:
Second Adam from above,
Reinstate us in Thy love.
Let us Thee, though lost, regain,
Thee, the Life, the inner man:
O, to all Thyself impart,
Formed in each believing heart.

—*Charles Wesley*

ABOUT THE POETS

John Ballenger lives in Mt. Vernon, Ohio, with his wife and two kids. He works and teaches creative writing at Mt. Vernon Nazarene University. He received his MFA from Ashland University and serves as the poetry editor for *Relief Journal*.

Daniel Bowman Jr. is the author of *A Plum Tree in Leatherstocking Country* and *Beggars in Heaven: A Novel*. A native of the Mohawk Valley in upstate New York, he lives with his wife, Bethany, and their two children in Indiana, where he teaches English and creative writing at Taylor University.

Drew Causey is the pastor of Worship and Arts at Hope Community Church in the Lawrenceburg/Frankfort area in Kentucky. He contributes regularly at Seedbed as both a writer and one of the hosts of *The Threshing Floor* Podcast.

Rod Dixon is a member of the Religious Society of Friends. His short stories have appeared in several journals, most recently *Red Rock Review*, *Euphony*, and *The Louisville Review*. For fun, he is the nonfiction editor of *Ontologica: A Journal of Art and Thought*. For money, he researches and develops manufacturing procedures for a nonprofit, serving the blind and visually impaired. He lives in Kentucky with his wife and two children.

Brad Fruhauff teaches English at Trinity International University and is editor-in-chief of *Relief: A Christian Literary Review*. His poems and reviews have appeared in *Relief*, *Rock & Sling*, *Catapult*, *Englewood Review of Books*, *Everyday Poems*, and *BooksAndCulture.com*. He and his family attend the Evanston Vineyard, where he has led small groups based on bluegrass gospel music, Christian disciplines, and contemporary spiritual poetry.

Amy L. George holds an MFA in creative writing from National University and is the author of *Desideratum*, *The Fragrance of Memory*, and *Sacred Fires and Ebullient Flames*. She lives in Texas with her husband and two cats and teaches at a private Christian university.

Dave Harrity is the founder and director of ANTLER, an organization devoted to teaching contemplative and creative practices. His most recent book is *Making Manifest: On Faith, Creativity, and the Kingdom at Hand*. He teaches at Campbellsville University and lives in Louisville, Kentucky, with his wife and children.

Amy McCann is the author of the poetry collection *Yes Thorn* (forthcoming from Tupelo Press, selected by Paisley Rekdal for the 2013 First/Second Book Award). Her poetry has appeared or will appear in *The Kenyon Review*, *The Gettysburg Review*, *West Branch*, and *Image*. Recent recognition includes a 2012–2013 McKnight Artist Fellowship in Poetry, a 2014 Minnesota State Arts Board Artist Initiative grant, and a 2014 Pushcart prize nomination from *Rock & Sling*. Raised in Illinois, she now lives in Minneapolis and teaches writing at the University of Northwestern–Saint Paul. She has an MFA from Eastern Washington University.

Jae Newman lives in Rochester, New York, with his wife and two daughters. He works at Monroe Community College where he teaches writing and literature courses. His poetry has been nominated for a Pushcart Prize. He holds an MFA in writing from Spalding University and is currently at work on a MA in theological studies at Northeastern Seminary.

Tania Runyan is the author of the poetry collections *Second Sky*, *A Thousand Vessels*, *Simple Weight*, and *Delicious Air*, which was awarded Book of the Year by the Conference on Christianity and Literature in 2007. Her book *How to Read a Poem,* an instructional guide based on Billy Collins's "Introduction to Poetry," was released in 2014. Her poems have appeared in many publications, including *Poetry, Image, Harvard Divinity Bulletin, The Christian Century, Atlanta Review, Indiana Review, Willow Springs, Nimrod,* and the anthology *In Fine Frenzy: Poets Respond to Shakespeare.* Tania was awarded an NEA Literature Fellowship in 2011.

Nicholas Samaras won The Yale Series of Younger Poets Award for his first book, *Hands of the Saddlemaker.* His new book, *American Psalm, World Psalm,* is now out with Ashland Poetry Press.

Ryan Strebeck lives in Sedan, New Mexico, with his wife, Amberly, and their three children. He is a Methodist pastor and a rancher who enjoys building just about anything—especially with hand tools. Ryan's stubborn streak and dogged work tendencies have earned him frequent comparisons to Woodrow F. Call of *Lonesome Dove.*

J. D. Walt, published author, songwriter, and poet, is the sower-in-chief for Seedbed Publishing. He lives in Franklin, Tennessee, with his wife, Tiffani, and their four children.

Isaac Watts *(1674-1748)* was an English Christian theologian and logician. A prolific and popular hymn writer, he is recognized as the Father of English Hymnody, credited with some seven hundred fifty hymns. Many of his hymns remain in use today and are sung around the world.

Charles Wesley *(1707-1788)* was an English leader of the Methodist movement and the younger brother of Methodist founder, John Wesley. He is remembered and celebrated for the more than six thousand hymns he wrote, a number of which are still sung across the world today.

David Wright teaches creative writing and American Literature at Monmouth College in Monmouth, Illinois. His poems have appeared in *Ecotone, Image, Hobart,* and many other places. His latest poetry collection is *The Small Books of Bach* (Wipf & Stock, 2014).

If you've enjoyed this Advent reader, please join us online at the Seedbed Daily Text (DailyText.Seedbed.com). Each day you will find a continuously unfolding passage of Scripture and a short reflection by J. D. Walt. The Twelve Day Celebration of Christmas will start on December 25.

NOT YET CHRISTMAS